ALL-TIME-FAVORITE RECIPES *From*

PENNSYLVANIA

COOKS

Dedication

For every cook who wants to create amazing
recipes from the great state of Pennsylvania.

Appreciation

Thanks to all our Pennsylvania cooks who shared their
delightful and delicious recipes with us!

Gooseberry Patch
An imprint of Globe Pequot
246 Goose Lane
Guilford, CT 06437
www.gooseberrypatch.com
1 800 854 6673

Copyright 2020, Gooseberry Patch
978-162093-399-2

Do you have a tried & true recipe... tip, craft or
memory that you'd like to see featured in a
Gooseberry Patch cookbook? Visit our website at
www.gooseberrypatch.com and follow the easy steps
to submit your favorite family recipe.

Or send them to us at:

Gooseberry Patch
PO Box 812
Columbus, OH 43216-0812

Don't forget to include the number of servings your
recipe makes, plus your name, address, phone
number and email address. If we select your recipe,
your name will appear right along with it...and you'll
receive a FREE copy of the book!

PENNSYLVANIA COOKS

ICONIC PENNSYLVANIA

You don't have to ring the Liberty Bell to appreciate the freedoms that were fought for after William Penn founded Pennsylvania. From Hershey Park to Heinz Stadium, one thing is for sure...the great state of Pennsylvania has paved the way with a rich history in both United States government and culinary affairs!

With the largest Amish community in the U.S., you can go to Lancaster County and watch the Amish drive horse-drawn carriages and plow their fields much in the same way as some of our ancestors. From there you can visit Gettysburg and see the place where President Lincoln delivered his famous speech...The Gettysburg Address.

One of the sweetest parts of Pennsylvania is in Hershey. At Hershey Park you can sample delicious candy at the world's largest chocolate factory!

However, it's easy for something savory to capture your sweet tooth...especially when it's in Piladelphia. The Philly Cheesesteak sandwich was created in the 1930s by Harry and Pat Olivien and kindled the inspiration for the many amazing sandwiches Pennsylvania holds claim to today!

In this collection from Pennsylvania cooks, you'll find a collection of mouthwatering recipes like: Perogie Caserole, Pennsylvania Dutch Scrapple, Philly Cheesesteaks, Meatball Hoagies and more!

OUR STORY

Back in 1984, our families were neighbors in little Delaware, Ohio. With small children, we wanted to do what we loved and stay home with the kids too. We had always shared a love of home cooking and so, **Gooseberry Patch** was born.

Almost immediately, we found a connection with our customers and it wasn't long before these friends started sharing recipes. Since then we've enjoyed publishing hundreds of cookbooks with your tried & true recipes.

We know we couldn't have done it without our friends all across the country and we look forward to continuing to build a community with you. Welcome to the **Gooseberry Patch** family!

JoAnn & Vickie

TABLE OF CONTENTS

CHAPTER ONE

Betsy Ross

Breakfasts

ENJOY THESE TASTY BREAKFAST
RECIPES THAT BRING YOU TO
THE TABLE WITH A HEARTY
"GOOD MORNING!" AND CARRY
YOU THROUGH THE DAY TO TACKLE
WHATEVER COMES YOUR WAY.

PENNSYLVANIA DUTCH SCRAPPLE

VIRGINIA WATSON
SCRANTON, PA

Squares of this savory dish are usually served for breakfast...but sometimes, it's great for dinner too.

1 lb. boneless pork loin, chopped
1 c. cornmeal
14-1/2 oz. can chicken broth
1/4 t. dried thyme
1/4 t. salt
1/2 c. all-purpose flour
1/4 t. pepper
2 T. oil
Optional: maple syrup

In a saucepan, cover pork with water; bring to a boil over medium heat. Simmer until fork-tender, about an hour; drain. Process in a food processor until minced. In a large saucepan over medium heat, combine pork, cornmeal, broth, thyme and salt; bring to a boil. Reduce heat and simmer, stirring constantly, for 2 minutes, or until mixture is very thick. Line a 9"x5" loaf pan with wax paper, letting paper extend above top of pan. Spoon pork mixture into pan; cover and chill for 4 hours to overnight. Unmold; cut into slices and set aside. On a plate, combine flour and pepper. Coat slices with flour mixture. In a large skillet, heat oil over medium heat; cook slices on both sides until golden. Drizzle with syrup, if desired.

Serves 12

JUST FOR FUN

The first daily newspaper was published in Philadelphia on September 21, 1784 by by Benjamin Franklin's older brother.

REUBEN BRUNCH CASSEROLE

LEONA KRIVDA
BELLE VERNON, PA

We like breakfast anytime, so I make this dish for dinner once in awhile too. Put it together in the morning, serve that night.

Arrange bread cubes in a greased 13"x9" baking pan. Layer corned beef over bread cubes; sprinkle with cheese. In a bowl, beat together eggs, milk and pepper; pour over top. Cover with aluminum foil and refrigerate for 8 hours to overnight. Bake, covered, at 350 degrees for 45 minutes. Uncover and bake an additional 10 minutes. Serve immediately.

Serves 6 to 8

- 10 slices rye bread, cut into 3/4-inch cubes
- 1-1/2 lbs. cooked corned beef, coarsely shredded
- 10-oz. pkg. Swiss cheese, shredded
- 6 eggs, lightly beaten
- 3 c. milk
- 1/4 t. pepper

MARINE CORPS BREAKFAST

MARILYN MILLER
FORT WASHINGTON, PA

From my dad's days in the U.S. Marine Corps...anyone with a hearty appetite will appreciate this old favorite!

In a large skillet over medium heat, brown and crumble ground beef with drippings and salt. Remove skillet from heat; let cool slightly. Mix in flour until all of the beef is covered. Return skillet to medium heat and stir in milk. Cook and stir until mixture comes to a boil and thickens; boil for at least one minute. Serve over toast.

Serves 8

- 1/2 lb. ground beef
- 1 T. bacon drippings
- 1/8 t. salt
- 3 T. all-purpose flour
- 2 c. milk
- salt and pepper to taste
- 8 slices white bread, toasted

BUBBLE BREAKFAST PIZZA

LINDA KILGORE
KITTANNING, PA

A quick, delicious breakfast that's a family favorite! Try it with crisp bacon instead of sausage too.

16-oz. pkg. ground pork breakfast sausage
1 doz. eggs
1/2 c. milk
1 T. butter
16-oz. tube refrigerated jumbo biscuits
8-oz. pkg. pasteurized process cheese spread, sliced

Brown sausage in a large skillet over medium heat; drain and set aside. Whisk together eggs and milk in a large bowl. Wipe out skillet; melt butter over low heat and add egg mixture. Cook and stir until eggs are lightly scrambled. While eggs are cooking, separate biscuits and press into a greased 13"x9" baking pan, forming a crust. Spoon scrambled eggs over biscuits; top with sausage and cheese. Bake, uncovered, at 375 degrees for 30 minutes, or until biscuits are set and cheese melts.

Serves 8

PAN-FRIED BREAKFAST POTATOES

VICKIE
GOOSEBERRY PATCH

A must with eggs for breakfast! Here's a hint...don't stir the potatoes very much. Just let them cook, turning occasionally.

3 russet potatoes, peeled, cubed and rinsed
3 T. butter or bacon drippings
salt and pepper to taste

Pat potato cubes dry; set aside. Melt butter or drippings in a large skillet over medium heat. Add potatoes and stir to coat. Season with salt and pepper. Cover and cook for 10 minutes. Uncover and cook for another 10 minutes, turning often, until crisp and golden on all sides.

Serves 3 to 4

BLUEBERRY CHEESE DANISH

JOANNA NICOLINE-HAUGHEY
BERWYN, PA

I make this special treat for my daughter's teachers. The school staff loves it...it's so simple but tastes like I have been baking all morning! Try it with cherry pie filling too.

Lightly grease a 13"x9" baking pan. Unroll one tube of crescent rolls and place in bottom of pan; set aside. In a bowl, blend cream cheese, egg yolk, sugar and vanilla; spread over crescent rolls. Spoon pie filling over cream cheese mixture. Unroll remaining crescent rolls and place on top. Whisk egg white in a cup until foamy; spread over crescents. Sprinkle with cinnamon-sugar. Bake at 350 degrees for 25 to 30 minutes. Cool completely; cut into squares.

Serves 10 to 12

2 8-oz. tubes refrigerated crescent rolls
2 8-oz. pkgs. cream cheese, softened
1 egg, separated
3/4 c. sugar
1 t. vanilla extract
21-oz. can blueberry pie filling
Garnish: cinnamon-sugar

JUST FOR FUN

Need a cup of coffee? The biggest coffee pot in Pennsylvania is The Coffee Pot, a building in the shape of ... you guessed it! Originally built in 1927 as a restaurant, the two-story building eventually fell into disrepair, but was restored to its original glory in 2004.

AUTUMN AMISH BAKED OATMEAL

KAREN SAMPSON
WAYMART, PA

My grandkids Silas and Eliza have enjoyed this tasty fall breakfast treat since they were toddlers. Especially when we top it with a splash of Grandpa's homemade maple syrup!

Optional: 1/2 c. diced apples, 1/2 c. raisins

1-1/2 c. long-cooking oats, uncooked

1/2 c. brown sugar, packed

1 egg, beaten

1/4 c. oil

1 c. milk

1 t. baking powder

1 t. cinnamon

Garnish: additional milk

Layer apples and/or raisins in the bottom of a greased 9"x9" baking pan, if using; set aside. Beat together remaining ingredients except garnish with a spoon. Pour oat mixture into pan. Bake, uncovered, at 300 degrees for 30 to 35 minutes. Serve topped with milk.

Serves 6

FRENCH TOASTWICHES

JUDY LANGE
IMPERIAL, PA

Kids love these banana-filled hot breakfast sandwiches...yum!

3 eggs, lightly beaten

1/3 c. milk

1 T. sugar

1/4 t. nutmeg

6 slices bread

1 to 2 T. butter, sliced

2 to 3 ripe bananas, sliced

Garnish: maple syrup, powdered sugar, honey or jelly

In a shallow bowl, combine eggs, milk, sugar and nutmeg; beat well. Dip each slice of bread into mixture until moistened on both sides. Melt butter on a griddle over medium heat. Add bread; cook until golden on both sides. To serve, arrange bananas over 3 French toast slices. Top with the remaining toast to make sandwiches. Serve hot, garnished as desired.

Serves 3

POTATO & EGG CASSEROLE

KAREN TATMAN
FAIRFIELD, PA

My staff at work is happy whenever I make breakfast for them. Swiss cheese & ham, Cheddar & bacon or Cheddar with Monterey Jack & sausage are all popular variations. You can also add finely chopped vegetables like broccoli, green and red peppers and tomatoes. Add the cut-up vegetables after you beat the eggs.

Place chopped or cubed meat in a greased 13"x9" baking pan; set aside. Beat eggs in a large bowl; stir in seasonings, potatoes and 1-1/2 cups cheese. Pour egg mixture over meat. Cover and bake at 350 degrees for 45 to 55 minutes, until a knife tip inserted near the center comes out clean. Sprinkle with remaining cheese; let stand 5 minutes before serving.

Serves 10

1 lb. cooked bacon, sausage or ham, chopped or cubed

1 doz. eggs

1 t. onion powder

1/4 t. garlic powder

1/4 t. paprika

salt and pepper to taste

2 c. potatoes, peeled, cooked and diced

2 c. favorite shredded cheese, divided

BREAKFAST BERRY PARFAIT

MICHELLE CASE
YARDLEY, PA

We like all kinds of berries, so we make this combining all of our favorites!

Layer half of the cereal and all of the yogurt in the 2 glasses. Add berries and top with remaining cereal.

Serves 2

1 c. bran & raisin cereal, divided

6-oz. container low-fat strawberry yogurt

1 c. strawberries, hulled and sliced

1/2 c. raspberries

1/4 c. blackberries

TOFFEE APPLE FRENCH TOAST

PATRICIA WISSLER
HARRISBURG, PA

This is so yummy and sweet! Make it the night before and pop it in the fridge...perfect for overnight weekend guests!

8 c. French bread, sliced into 1-inch cubes and divided

2 Granny Smith apples, peeled, cored and chopped

8-oz. pkg. cream cheese, softened

3/4 c. brown sugar, packed

1/4 c. sugar

1-3/4 c. milk, divided

2 t. vanilla extract, divided

1/2 c. toffee or almond brickle baking bits

5 eggs, beaten

Place half the bread cubes in a greased 13"x9" baking pan; top with apples and set aside. In a medium bowl, beat cream cheese, sugars, 1/4 cup milk and one teaspoon vanilla until smooth. Stir in baking bits and spread over apples. Top with remaining bread cubes. In a separate bowl, beat eggs with remaining milk and vanilla; pour over bread. Cover and refrigerate for 8 hours to overnight. Remove from refrigerator 30 minutes before baking. Uncover and bake at 350 degrees for 35 to 45 minutes, until a knife inserted near the center comes out clean.

Serves 8

PRESENTATION

When guests are coming for brunch, a little kitchen prep the night before is really helpful. Whisk up eggs for scrambling, stir together dry ingredients for waffles and lay out tableware ahead of time...in the morning, just tie on your prettiest apron and you'll be a relaxed hostess!

SUNDAY BRUNCH QUICHE

AMY DAILY
MORRISVILLE, PA

This is a wonderful dish. I used to make it on Sundays when my parents had brunch with my husband & me. It was a great way to get veggies into a dish without my dad picking them out! Since Dad has passed, I make it a lot more often, instead of just on special occasions. It has become one of my mom's favorite meals that I make for her...she always takes home the leftovers. I like to serve this with a fruit salad.

Press pie crust into a 9" pie plate; set aside. Brown sausage in a skillet over medium heat. Drain; transfer to a large bowl and set aside. Wipe out skillet with a paper towel. Add butter and oil to skillet. Add mushrooms; cover and sauté for 3 to 5 minutes. Add onion and red pepper; cook an additional 8 to 10 minutes. Add vegetables and cheese to sausage; mix well. Spoon into pie crust and set aside. In a separate bowl, whisk together remaining ingredients. Pour into pie crust to cover sausage mixture. Bake, uncovered, at 375 degrees for 40 to 45 minutes, until a knife tip inserted in the center tests clean. Let stand 5 minutes; cut into wedges.

Serves 6 to 8

9-inch pie crust

3/4 lb. Italian pork
  sausage link, casing
  removed

2 T. butter

1 T. oil

8-oz. pkg. sliced
  mushrooms

1/2 sweet onion, diced

1 c. red pepper, diced

8-oz. pkg. shredded
  Colby-Jack cheese

5 eggs, beaten

3/4 c. half-and-half

1/2 t. dry mustard

1/4 t. salt

1/8 t. pepper

KITCHEN TIP

Add 20 to 30% more flavor to your cup of coffee! Simply wet the paper filter before brewing.

BAKED CINNAMON-APPLE FRENCH TOAST CASSEROLE

BETHI HENDRICKSON
DANVILLE, PA

*A wonderful addition to a family brunch or a retreat with friends.
Wonderful with a cup of coffee, good company and lots of smiles.*

1 c. brown sugar, packed
1/2 c. butter, melted
4 t. cinnamon, divided
1/2 t. allspice
4 apples, peeled, cored and thinly sliced
3/4 c. sweetened dried cranberries
1/2 c. chopped pecans, toasted
1 loaf French baguette, sliced 1/2-inch thick
6 eggs, beaten
1-1/2 c. milk
1 T. vanilla extract
1/4 t. nutmeg
Garnish: whipped cream

Combine brown sugar, butter, 2 teaspoons cinnamon and allspice in a large bowl; mix well. Add apples and toss to coat. Spread apple mixture evenly in a 13"x9" baking pan sprayed with non-stick vegetable spray. Sprinkle cranberries and pecans over apples. Arrange bread slices on top until completely covered; set aside. In a separate bowl, whisk together eggs, milk, vanilla, remaining cinnamon and nutmeg. Pour evenly over bread slices. Cover pan with aluminum foil and refrigerate for 6 to 24 hours. Bake at 375 degrees for 40 minutes. Remove foil; bake an additional 10 minutes, or until lightly golden. Let cool 5 minutes. Cut into squares; add a dollop of whipped cream.

Serves 8 to 10

BROWN SUGAR-GLAZED BACON

CAITLIN HAGY
WEST CHESTER, PA

A delicious addition to any autumn breakfast table.

1 lb. bacon
1/3 c. brown sugar, packed
1 t. all-purpose flour
1/2 c. pecans, finely chopped

Place a wire rack over a baking sheet. Arrange bacon slices on rack, close together but not overlapping. In a bowl, combine remaining ingredients and sprinkle evenly over bacon. Bake at 350 degrees for about 30 minutes, until bacon is crisp and glazed. Drain on paper towels before serving.

Serves 6 to 8

QUICK JAM DANISHES

LISA ASHTON
ASTON, PA

You'll love these easy-to-make breakfast treats. They're yummy with strawberry, apricot or peach jam...you could even make a batch with several different flavors of jam!

Unroll crescent roll dough and separate into triangles. Place one teaspoon cream cheese on the long side of each triangle, mashing lightly; top the cream cheese with one teaspoon jam. Roll up triangle, starting with the long side, to secure cream cheese and jam inside. Pull over the point, pinching sides to seal. Place on an ungreased baking sheet; sprinkle with sugar. Bake at 375 degrees for 18 to 20 minutes, until golden.

8-oz. tube refrigerated crescent rolls

8 t. cream cheese, softened and divided

8 t. favorite-flavor jam, divided

Garnish: coarse sugar

Makes 8 servings

COZY BREAKFAST CASSEROLE

ROBIN ROBERTSON
EAST STROUDSBURG, PA

A hearty, savory hot dish that I always made on Christmas Eve to pop in the oven on Christmas morning...now that my boys are older, they still request this every year.

Combine eggs, milk and mustard in a large bowl; mix well and set aside. Layer bread cubes, sausage and cheese in a greased 13"x9" baking pan. Pour egg mixture over top; refrigerate overnight. Bake, covered, at 350 degrees for 45 minutes. Uncover and bake for an additional 10 minutes.

4 eggs, beaten

2 c. milk

1/2 t. dry mustard

6 slices bread, cubed

1 lb. breakfast sausage links, browned, drained and sliced

8-oz. pkg. shredded Cheddar cheese

Serves 4 to 6

CHAPTER TWO

Mount Mile-High
Salads

TOSS TOGETHER GREAT TASTE
AND HEALTHY GOODNESS TO
MAKE MARKET-FRESH, SATISFYING
AND TASTY SALADS THAT ARE
PACKED WITH FULL-ON FLAVOR.

JUDY'S POTATO SALAD

CHARLOTTE SMITH
TYRONE, PA

This recipe was given to me by a friend who goes to our church. She has always been someone that I know I can count on. It's the best potato salad in the world...once you try this recipe, you will surely agree!

6 potatoes, peeled and cubed

2 eggs, lightly beaten

2/3 c. water

1/3 c. vinegar

1/2 c. plus 3 T. sugar

1 T. all-purpose flour

1/4 t. dry mustard

1 to 2 t. celery seed

4 to 6 T. mayonnaise-style salad dressing

Cover potatoes with water in a large saucepan. Cook over medium high heat until tender; drain and transfer to a serving bowl. Meanwhile, in a separate saucepan, combine remaining ingredients except salad dressing. Bring to a boil over medium heat, stirring constantly. Add salad dressing; mix well. Remove from heat and pour over potatoes. Mix well; cover and chill until serving time.

Serves 8 to 10

TART APPLE SALAD

LEONA KRIVDA
BELLE VERNON, PA

My husband really likes this nice fall salad. I always serve it at Thanksgiving.

Toss together apples, grapes, celery and walnuts in a large serving bowl; sprinkle with sugar. Stir in salad dressing; mix well. Cover and chill until serving time. Fold in whipped cream and cranberries just before serving.

Serves 10 to 12

6 tart crisp apples, peeled, cored and chopped

1-1/2 c. seedless red grapes, halved

1 c. celery, finely chopped

1/2 c. chopped walnuts

1/4 c. sugar

1 T. mayonnaise-style salad dressing

1/2 pt. whipping cream, whipped

1/4 c. sweetened dried cranberries

KITCHEN TIP

A fast-fix veggie dip that's yummy! Stir together 1-1/4 cups sour cream with 1/2 cup mayonnaise and a one-ounce package of dry onion soup mix. Spoon dip into a serving bowl and garnish with minced chives.

PEAR HARVEST SALAD

PEAR HARVEST SALAD

LORI RITCHEY
DENVER, PA

I love a sweet, crunchy salad with fruit and nuts. This is a delicious combination that's just right for any autumn meal.

8-oz. pkg. mixed salad greens

15-oz. can pear halves, drained and 1/3 c. juice reserved

1/2 c. chopped walnuts or pecans, toasted

1/4 red onion, thinly sliced and separated into rings

2/3 c. blue cheese salad dressing

Place salad greens in a large salad bowl. Top with pear halves, nuts and onion. Stir reserved pear juice into salad dressing; drizzle over salad. Serve immediately.

Serves 6 to 8

KITCHEN TIP

Stash bags of fresh salad greens in the fridge along with chopped veggies and even crispy bacon left from breakfast. Toss with dressing for a salad ready in a flash!

ENSINGTON LATROBE PARK MEADVILLE

STRAWBERRY-CRANBERRY SALAD

CHARLOTTE SMITH
TYRONE, PA

We serve this salad for just about every holiday year 'round...it's so good you can enjoy it anytime! It needs to chill for quite awhile, so be sure to start a day ahead.

In a large bowl, mix together gelatin mix and boiling water; stir until dissolved. Add remaining ingredients; mix well. Cover and chill for 12 to 24 hours. Transfer to a serving bowl; stir before serving.

Serves 20.

2 3-oz. pkg's. strawberry gelatin mix
2 c. boiling water
20-oz. can crushed pineapple, drained and 1/2 c. juice reserved
16-oz. can whole-berry cranberry sauce
10-oz. pkg. frozen sliced strawberries, thawed
1 c. chopped walnuts

TOMATO-MOZZARELLA SALAD

JOANNA NICOLINE-HAUGHEY
BERWYN, PA

I remember Mom serving this simple salad in the summertime, made with fresh ingredients from Dad's wonderful garden full of sun-ripe red tomatoes, cucumbers, green peppers and herbs. What great memories!

Mix tomatoes, cucumber, cheese and basil together in a serving bowl. Drizzle with oil and toss to mix; sprinkle with salt and pepper.

Serves 4

4 tomatoes, cubed
1 cucumber, sliced
1 c. mozzarella cheese, cubed
1 T. fresh basil, chopped
1/4 c. extra virgin olive oil
salt and pepper to taste

CHRISTMAS CELEBRATION SALAD

CYNDY DESTEFANO
MERCER, PA

New to our holiday menu last year, this salad has quickly become a favorite. The cranberries add that festive flavor and colorful touch... perfect for the Christmas table.

1 t. salt

2 apples, peeled, cored and chopped

4 c. mixed salad greens

1/2 c. sweetened dried cranberries

1/2 c. glazed almonds

1/2 c. crumbled blue cheese or Gorgonzola cheese

CELEBRATION DRESSING:

1/3 c. cider vinegar

1/3 c. honey

1 t. cinnamon

1/2 t. salt

1/4 c. olive oil

Dissolve salt in a medium bowl of warm water; add apples to water and let stand several minutes. In a serving bowl, combine remaining ingredients. Drain apples; add to salad. Drizzle Celebration Dressing over top; toss before serving.

Celebration Dressing: In a small bowl, whisk together all ingredients except oil. Add oil in a slow stream, whisking constantly, until mixture is smooth. Dressing may be prepared up to 2 weeks ahead of time and stored in the refrigerator in an airtight container.

Serves 4

CRUNCHY PEA & PEANUT SALAD

MARCIA SHAFFER
CONNEAUT LAKE, PA

We enjoy this salad when we're watching the game on television.

Combine all ingredients in a bowl; mix well. Cover and chill until ready to serve.

Makes 8 to 10 servings

2 10-oz. pkg's. frozen peas
14-oz. can Spanish peanuts
3/4 c. sour cream
4 t. mayonnaise

FRUITY PICNIC SALAD

BARBARA ENCABABIAN
EASTON, PA

This fruit-filled salad is scrumptious, and it looks so pretty in a glass serving dish.

In a 4-quart glass serving dish, combine oranges and undrained pineapple, fruit cocktail and peaches. Add remaining fruit; set aside. Prepare gelatin mix according to package directions; let cool. Pour over fruit and stir. Cover and refrigerate overnight.

Makes 6 to 8 servings

2 11-oz. cans mandarin oranges, drained
20-oz. can pineapple chunks
16-oz. can fruit cocktail
15-oz. can sliced peaches
3 bananas, sliced
1 pt. strawberries, hulled and sliced
3-oz. pkg. raspberry gelatin mix

KATHLEEN'S BLT SALAD

KATHLEEN HARDEN
LATROBE, PA

I used to make stuffed tomatoes, but they always seemed so time-consuming so I came up with this salad version. It's also a wonderful, tasty way to use up those healthy, fresh tomatoes from the garden!

1 to 2 T. mayonnaise
1 t. vinegar
1/8 t. seafood seasoning
1/4 head iceberg lettuce, torn into bite-size pieces
2 tomatoes, cut into wedges
1/2 c. bacon, crisply cooked and crumbled
1/2 c. shredded Cheddar cheese

Whisk together mayonnaise, vinegar and seasoning. Set aside. Arrange lettuce and tomatoes on salad plates. Top with bacon and cheese. Drizzle with dressing. Toss before serving.

Serves 2

BONUS IDEA

Spice up your meal planning with some new ideas when you host a recipe swap party! Invite friends to bring a favorite casserole along with enough recipe cards for each guest. While everyone is enjoying the potluck of scrumptious food, collect the recipe cards, make a stack for everyone, and hand out when the party is over.

BEST PENNSYLVANIA DUTCH POTATO SALAD

BETHI HENDRICKSON
DANVILLE, PA

Our family lived away from home while my husband Brian served in the Army. Whenever I felt homesick for central Pennsylvania, I would make this yummy potato salad. It was always a fantastic addition to our evening supper and made me feel a little closer to our hometown.

Cover potatoes with water in a stockpot. Cook over medium heat until tender, about 15 minutes; drain. Immediately run cold water over potatoes; cool and set aside. In a blender, combine bacon, reserved drippings and remaining ingredients except celery and garnish. Process until well mixed; pour into a saucepan. Cook over medium heat until thickened and bubbly, whisking frequently. Combine potatoes and celery in a large bowl. Pour hot mixture over top and toss to mix. Cover and refrigerate for several hours before serving. Garnish with parsley.

Serves 8 to 10

6 to 8 potatoes, peeled and cubed

1 lb. bacon, crisply cooked, crumbled and 2 T. drippings reserved

2 eggs, beaten

1 c. milk

1 c. water

3/4 c. vinegar

3/4 c. sugar or calorie-free powdered sweetener

3 T. all-purpose flour

1/8 t. pepper

3 stalks celery, diced

Garnish: chopped fresh parsley

MOM'S FAMOUS
POTATO SALAD

CHRISTINA MAMULA
ALIQUIPPA, PA

*This was Mom's specialty. She made it only during the holidays.
At times, I think we were more excited about her potato salad at
Christmas than the gifts from Santa!*

6 to 7 lbs. potatoes,
  peeled and cubed

1 doz. eggs, hard-boiled,
  peeled and chopped

1-1/2 c. celery, chopped

1 c. onion, chopped

2 t. vinegar

2-1/2 c. mayonnaise-type
  salad dressing

2-1/2 T. mustard

2 t. dill pickle juice

3/4 c. sugar

1/3 c. milk

In a large stockpot over high heat, cover potatoes
with water and bring to a boil. Cook for 20 to 25
minutes, until potatoes are tender. Drain, but do not
rinse. Transfer potatoes to a large serving bowl;
allow to cool. Add eggs, celery and onion. In a
separate bowl, whisk together remaining ingredients.
Pour over potato mixture; mix well. Cover and chill
before serving.

Serves 10 to 12

FAJITA & BOWTIES SALAD BOWL

JEN STOUT
BLANDON, PA

A spicy twist on pasta salad.

Combine lime juice and spices in a food processor or blender. Process until almost smooth; drizzle in oil and process until blended. Set aside. In a large bowl, combine beans, corn, salsa, tomatoes, pasta and lime juice mixture; toss to combine. Gently mix in tortilla chips and cheese.

Serves 4

1/4 c. lime juice
1 T. ground cumin
1/2 t. chili powder
1/2 c. fresh cilantro, chopped
1/2 c. olive oil
15-oz. can black beans, drained and rinsed
11-oz. can corn, drained
1 c. salsa
2 tomatoes, chopped
8-oz. pkg. bowtie pasta, cooked
2 c. tortilla chips, crushed
1 c. shredded Cheddar cheese

SUMMER TORTELLINI SALAD

JEN STOUT
BLANDON, PA

Include any favorite veggies...a garnish of tomato wedges or orange slices and parsley sprigs is nice.

8-oz. pkg. cheese
tortellini, cooked and
cooled

1 tomato, chopped

3 to 4 slices hard
salami, thinly sliced
lengthwise

3 to 4 mushrooms, sliced

4 to 5 Kalamata olives,
pitted and chopped

1/2-inch thick slice mild
Cheddar cheese, cut
into 1/2-inch cubes

1/2-inch thick slice
mozzarella cheese, cut
into 1/2-inch cubes

1/2-inch thick slice
provolone cheese, cut
into 1/2-inch cubes

1/4 c. olive oil

1 clove garlic, finely
minced

1/4 t. garlic salt

1/8 t. pepper

2 to 3 T. cider vinegar

Optional: 1 t. red pepper
flakes

In a large bowl, combine tortellini, tomato, salami, mushrooms, olives and cheeses; set aside. Whisk together oil, garlic, garlic salt, pepper, vinegar and red pepper flakes, if using, until thoroughly mixed. Pour over the salad; mix well. Refrigerate for a few hours to overnight.

Serves 8

SUMMER SPINACH SALAD WITH FETA

MICHELLE MATUIZEK
SPRINGDALE, PA

When friends are coming over for lunch or dinner, "wow" them with this summer salad!

Combine first 5 ingredients in a large salad bowl; gently toss. Add dressing to taste; sprinkle with croutons.

Serves 7

9-oz. pkg. baby spinach

1-qt. container strawberries, hulled and sliced

2 c. blackberries

10-oz. pkg. chopped walnuts

2 8-oz. pkgs. crumbled feta cheese

16-oz. bottle raspberry-walnut vinaigrette

Garnish: 6-oz. pkg. croutons

JUST FOR FUN

In 1946, Philadelphia became home to the first computer.

CHAPTER THREE

Good as Gettysburg

Soups & Sandwiches

GATHER 'ROUND THE TABLE

TOGETHER WITH FAMILY & FRIENDS

TO COZY UP WITH A BOWL OF

HEARTY SOUP OR MAKE A TASTY

SANDWICH PERFECT FOR PACK'N

IN THE YUMMINESS FOR A BUSY

DAY IN PENNSYLVANIA.

BACON CHEESY HOT DOGS

DENISE EVANS
MOOSIC, PA

Raising seven children, my mom figured out ways to serve a hot meal every night. This is a delicious, affordable recipe...my twist is the cheese over the bacon. Mom only used bacon. Either way, they are great. Serve with French fries.

8 to 10 hot dogs
8 to 10 thin slices bacon
8 to 10 slices of sharp wite or american cheese, halved
8 to 10 hot dog rolls, split and warmed
Optional: catsup

Slice hot dogs down the center, but not all the way through. Place a bacon slice in the center of each hot dog; place on a broiler pan. Broil until bacon is almost browned. Remove from oven; top each slice of bacon with 2 half-slices of cheese. Broil for up to one minute, until cheese is melted. Place hot dogs in rolls; top with catsup, if desired.

Serves 4 to 5

SOUTH-OF-THE-BORDER TURKEY BURGERS

PATRICIA FLAK
ERIE, PA

For everybody who thinks turkey burgers are tasteless, give these a try...I get requests for them all the time! Serve on your favorite hamburger buns.

Combine all ingredients in a bowl. Mix well and shape into 4 patties; set aside. Spray an aluminum foil-lined broiler pan with non-stick vegetable spray. Place patties on pan. Broil for 5 to 6 minutes on each side, to desired doneness.

Serves 4

1 lb. lean ground turkey breast
1/2 red pepper, chopped
1/2 t. ground cumin
1/2 t. chili powder
1/8 t. hot pepper sauce

DINNERTIME CONVERSATION

Pittsburgh has over 300 sets of city-maintained steps. If they were stacked on top of each other, they would reach over 26,000 feet high...that's higher than a lot of the Himalayan Mountains!

SLOPPY JOE POCKET PIES

MEL CHENCHARICK
JULIAN, PA

*Need something quick to take for the kids to eat after the game?
They'll love these yummy little pockets!*

2 lbs. ground beef chuck

1 onion, chopped

16-oz. can Sloppy Joe sauce

1-1/2 t. garlic powder

6 9-inch pie crusts

1 c. shredded Cheddar cheese

1 egg yolk, lightly beaten

In a large skillet, brown beef and onion over medium-high heat; drain. Stir in sauce and garlic powder. Reduce heat to low; simmer for 20 minutes. Remove from heat; cool slightly. Meanwhile, on a lightly floured surface, unroll pie crusts. With a 5-inch round cutter, cut 5 circles from each crust, re-rolling dough as necessary. Spoon 2 tablespoons beef mixture into the center of each circle; top with 1-1/2 teaspoons cheese. Lightly brush edges of circles with egg yolk; fold over to enclose filling. Crimp edges with a fork to seal. Place pies on lightly greased baking sheets. Bake at 400 degrees for 20 minutes, or until golden. Best if served immediately.

Makes 2-1/2 dozen

LAUREL PIZZA BURGERS

DEBBY HARDISKY
NEW CASTLE, PA

This recipe was given to me by Donna Gentile, my best friend for many years. Our children attended elementary school together and loved these mini pizzas that were served in the cafeteria. All the kids couldn't wait to get one!

Brown beef in a skillet over medium heat; drain. Stir in remaining ingredients except buns. Simmer over low heat for about 10 minutes, until cheese melts. Separate buns and arrange, cut-side up, on an ungreased baking sheet. Spoon beef mixture onto buns. Bake, uncovered, at 350 degrees for about 20 minutes, until golden.

Serves 8

1 lb. ground beef

1/2 lb. bologna, ground
  or very finely chopped

1-1/2 c. pasteurized
  process cheese spread,
  shredded

1-1/2 c. spaghetti sauce

1 t. dried parsley

1/4 t. dried oregano

8 sandwich buns, split

PRESENTATION

Attach a strand of cool burning light bulbs to the underside of a patio table umbrella or along a fence to create an enchanting effect.

AUNTIE B'S HAMBURGER BBQ

BETHI HENDRICKSON
DANVILLE, PA

My Aunt Barb used to make this recipe all the time when I was a kid. Now I make it for my family. It can be made ahead or even frozen for busy evenings. It is a family favorite!

1 lb. ground beef

Optional: 1/2 c. onion, chopped

1/2 c. catsup

3 to 4 T. brown sugar, packed

2 T. Worcestershire sauce

2 T. water

1 T. white vinegar

1 T. mustard

8 hamburger buns, split

Optional: 8 slices cheese

In a skillet over medium heat, brown beef with onion, if using; drain. In a small bowl, combine remaining ingredients except buns and cheese. Whisk until smooth; pour over beef mixture. Reduce heat to low; simmer for 15 to 20 minutes, stirring occasionally. Serve on hamburger buns, topped with cheese, if desired.

Serves 8

THE BEST CHICKEN NOODLE SOUP

EVELYN BELCHER
MONROETON, PA

My daughter gave me this recipe years ago... now it's my favorite!

Cook noodles according to package directions; drain and set aside. Meanwhile, combine broth, salt and poultry seasoning in a very large pot; bring to a boil over medium heat. Stir in vegetables; reduce heat, cover and simmer for 15 minutes, or until vegetables are tender. Combine cornstarch with cold water in a small bowl; gradually add to soup, stirring constantly until thickened. Stir in chicken and noodles; heat through, about 5 to 10 minutes.

Serves 8 to 10

16-oz. pkg. thin egg noodles, uncooked
12 c. chicken broth
1-1/2 t. salt
1 t. poultry seasoning
1 c. celery, chopped
1 c. onion, chopped
1 c. carrot, peeled and chopped
1/3 c. cornstarch
1/4 c. cold water
4 c. cooked chicken, diced

HEARTY HAMBURGER VEGGIE SOUP

LORI RITCHEY
DENVER, PA

Every Christmas, our church presents a Living Nativity scene. Several ladies and gentlemen of our congregation bring crocks of soup to keep the actors warm when they are a part of the scenes outside. Everyone enjoys the food & fellowship in the church kitchen...this soup has become a favorite! The recipe can easily be doubled to feed more.

1 lb. lean ground beef
1 T. garlic powder
14-1/2 oz. can Italian-seasoned diced tomatoes
2 10-1/2 oz. cans beef broth
16-oz. pkg. frozen soup vegetables
1 T. onion powder
1 t. pepper
1 T. Worcestershire sauce

In a large stockpot over medium heat, brown beef with garlic powder; drain. Add tomatoes with juice and remaining ingredients; bring to a boil. Reduce heat to low; simmer for about 45 minutes, stirring occasionally.

Serves 6 to 8

FRENCH-FRIED TOMATO SANDWICHES

JODY SOMOGYI
ALLENTOWN, PA

You've never tasted anything like these yummy sandwiches before! The recipe was handed down from my grandmother.

In a bowl, combine sour cream, cheese and herbs. Season with lemon juice, salt and pepper; set aside. Using half of butter, spread butter on one side of each bread slice. Spread sour cream mixture on the buttered side of 4 slices, leaving a 1/4-inch border. Place a slice of tomato on each slice of buttered bread. Arrange remaining bread slices on the tomatoes, butter-side down. Press sandwiches together slightly. In a shallow dish, beat eggs and milk together; season with more salt and pepper. Melt remaining butter in a large heavy skillet over medium heat. Dip both sides of each sandwich into milk mixture; allow sandwiches to soak up milk mixture for a few seconds before transferring them to skillet. Cook sandwiches for 2 to 3 minutes on each side, until crisp and golden. Drain sandwiches on paper towels; cut into quarters and serve.

Serves 4

1/2 c. sour cream

1/2 c. Gruyère cheese, grated

2 T. fresh dill, snipped

2 T. fresh chives, snipped

lemon juice to taste

salt and white pepper to taste

3 T. butter, softened and divided

8 slices white or wheat bread, crusts trimmed

2 ripe tomatoes, sliced 1/4-inch thick

2 eggs

1/4 c. milk

BROWN SUGAR BARBECUES

KATHY MAJESKE
DENVER, PA

There are many recipes for making barbecues, but this one has been in my family for as long as I can remember. It's a time-saver...there's no need to brown the ground beef first.

1 c. water
3/4 c. catsup
2 T. brown sugar, packed
1 onion, chopped
2 T. mustard
1 T. chili powder
2 t. salt
1 t. pepper
2 lbs. lean ground beef
12 sandwich buns, split

In a large saucepan, mix all ingredients except ground beef and buns. Bring to a boil over medium heat. Add uncooked beef; simmer for about 20 to 30 minutes. Spoon onto buns.

Serves 12

CREAMY VEGGIE SANDWICHES

KELLY ALDERSON
ERIE, PA

My kids like this meatless sandwich spread very much. Sometimes we'll change it up by adding diced cucumber, thinly sliced radish or whatever else is on hand in the fridge.

Place broccoli in a small microwave-safe bowl; add one tablespoon water. Cover with plastic wrap. Microwave for 3 minutes, or until crisp-tender. Drain well and cool; chop finely. In a separate bowl, combine broccoli, remaining vegetables and ricotta cheese. Spread mixture on 2 slices bread; top with remaining bread.

Serves 2

1/4 c. broccoli flowerets
1/4 c. red pepper, diced
1/2 c. carrot, peeled and finely shredded
1-1/4 c. ricotta cheese
4 slices whole-wheat or country-style bread, crusts trimmed

PRESENTATION

For take-home gifts, fill Mason jars with your own special savory sauce. Tie on a recipe card and a BBQ brush with a bit of jute...your guests will love it!

DARCI'S PIZZA BURGERS

**DARCI HEATON
WOODBURY, PA**

Very simple to make and budget-friendly, this slow-cooker recipe can be doubled or tripled for a potluck or party. Make it your own with any spices and extra touches you like. Yummy!

1 lb. ground beef
salt, pepper, onion
   powder and
garlic powder to taste
1 to 1-1/2 15-oz. jars pizza
   sauce
1 c. shredded mozzarella
   cheese
3-oz. pkg. pepperoni,
   diced
1 t. Italian seasoning
6 to 8 sandwich buns,
   split
6 to 8 slices mozzarella
   cheese

Brown beef in a skillet over medium heat; drain. Season with salt, pepper, onion powder and garlic powder. Spoon beef into a slow cooker. Add desired amount of pizza sauce, shredded cheese and pepperoni; stir well. Cover and cook on low setting for 4 hours, or until hot and bubbly. About 30 minutes before serving, sprinkle in Italian seasoning; stir. To serve, spoon onto buns; top with a cheese slice.

Serves 6 to 8

JUST FOR FUN

The oldest gas station in the U.S. is located in Altoona...Reighard's Gas Station opened in 1909, and is still in business today.

KAY'S BACON-TOMATO SANDWICHES

CHERYL LAGLER
ZIONSVILLE, PA

When my children were young, my friend Kay and I would get together monthly to visit and have lunch. Kay first prepared this sandwich and I knew I had a quick & delicious dinner recipe for my family. The flavors blend together in a truly scrumptious sandwich!

Combine mayonnaise and mustard; spread evenly over cut side of rolls. Layer remaining ingredients on rolls in order given. Close sandwiches and place on an ungreased baking sheet. Bake at 350 degrees for 5 to 8 minutes, or until cheese melts.

Serves 4

1/3 c. mayonnaise

1 T. mustard

4 onion rolls, split

8 slices bacon, crisply cooked

4 slices tomato

12 slices red onion

12 slices cucumber

8 slices Cheddar cheese

RED PEPPER & CHICKEN BAGELS

JANICE PIGGA
BETHLEHEM, PA

This is a quick recipe that's perfect whenever time is short.

2 boneless, skinless
  chicken breasts
1/8 t. salt
1/8 t. pepper
1/4 c. balsamic vinegar
3 T. Worcestershire
  sauce
2 bagels, split
2 slices fresh mozzarella
  cheese
2 slices roasted red
  pepper

Place chicken between 2 pieces of wax paper; pound until thin. Sprinkle with salt and pepper. In a bowl, combine vinegar and Worcestershire sauce; marinate chicken 10 to 15 minutes. Drain and discard marinade. Place chicken on a lightly greased grill or in a skillet over medium heat. Cook and turn chicken until golden and juices run clear, about 20 minutes. Place chicken on bagel halves; top with cheese, pepper slices and remaining bagel halves. Arrange on an ungreased baking sheet and bake at 350 degrees until cheese is melted, about 5 to 10 minutes.

Serves 2

ROASTED VEGGIE ROLLS

BECKY TETLAK
MOUNTAIN TOP, PA

Here's a super recipe for your bushel of zucchini!

Arrange mushrooms and zucchini on a greased baking sheet. Bake at 400 degrees for 10 minutes. Add tomato to the baking sheet and continue baking 15 minutes longer, turning vegetables halfway through baking time. In a food processor, combine remaining ingredients except rolls and cheese; pulse to blend. Spread artichoke mixture over split rolls; layer with vegetables and cheese.

Serves 2

2 portabella mushroom caps
1 zucchini, thinly sliced
1 tomato, sliced
6-oz. jar artichoke hearts, drained
1 clove garlic, minced
1 T. olive oil
1/2 t. lemon juice
1/8 t. kosher salt
pepper to taste
2 multi-grain rolls, split
1/4 c. crumbled feta cheese

CHEESEBURGER ROLL-UPS

KELLY ALDERSON
ERIE, PA

Made before we ever leave to go camping, these super-simple sandwiches disappear just as soon as our tent is set up!

2 lbs. ground beef
3/4 c. soft bread crumbs
1/2 c. onion, minced
2 eggs, beaten
1-1/2 t. salt
1-1/2 t. pepper
12-oz. pkg. shredded Cheddar cheese
6 to 8 sandwich buns, split
Garnish: catsup, mustard and lettuce

In a large bowl, combine beef, bread crumbs, onion, eggs, salt and pepper; mix well. Pat out into an 18-inch by 14-inch rectangle on a piece of wax paper. Spread cheese over meat, leaving a 3/4-inch border around edges. Roll up jelly-roll fashion starting at short edge. Press ends to seal. Place on a lightly greased 15"x10" jelly-roll pan. Bake at 350 degrees for one hour, or until internal temperature on a meat thermometer reaches 160 degrees. Let stand for at least 10 minutes before slicing. Slice and serve on buns; garnish as desired.

Serves 6 to 8

JUST FOR FUN

In 1909, Forbes Field, the first baseball stadium was built in Pittsburgh.

MOM'S SANDWICH SPREAD

KAREN VASICAK
SWOYERSVILLE, PA

My mother often made these sandwiches for us as kids...they're great to take on trips and enjoy with a bag of potato chips. There are a lot of sandwich spread recipes; however, Mom's recipe is different because it includes a green pepper...it adds a tasty spin to the usual sandwich spread flavor.

Combine all ingredients except salad dressing and bread in a meat grinder. Process to desired consistency. Stir in salad dressing to taste. Assemble sandwiches.

Serves 8 to 12

- 1 lb. bologna, coarsely chopped
- 1 onion, coarsely chopped
- 16-oz. jar sweet pickles, drained and coarsely chopped
- 1 green pepper, coarsely chopped
- mayonnaise-style salad dressing to taste
- 1 loaf sliced white bread

FAMILY-FAVORITE PORK BARBECUE

GLADYS BREHM
QUAKERTOWN, PA

A family recipe handed down by generations. I tried different ingredients until I liked the taste. The sauce is also good made with ground beef, browned and combined with the other ingredients.

2 to 3-lb. pork butt roast
1 c. celery, chopped
3/4 c. onion, chopped
1-1/2 c. catsup
1/4 c. brown sugar, packed
1/4 c. cider vinegar
1 T. mustard
hamburger buns, split

Place roast in a large slow cooker; do not add anything. Cover and cook on low setting for 6 to 8 hours, until well done. Remove roast; drain juices from slow cooker. Return roast to slow cooker; shred with 2 forks. Stir in remaining ingredients except buns. Cover and cook on low setting for an additional 4 to 6 hours, until flavors are blended and vegetables are tender. Serve pork mixture on buns.

Serves 10 to 12

FIRE-ROASTED TOMATO & SAUSAGE GRINDERS

MEL CHENCHARICK
JULIAN, PA

These grinders are just the best! Made in a slow cooker, they're ready when you get home from work.

Place sausage links in a 6-quart slow cooker; set aside. For sauce, combine diced and crushed tomatoes with juice, vinegar, garlic and seasonings. Mix well; spoon over sausage links. Cover and cook on low setting for 6 to 8 hours, or on high setting for 3 to 4 hours. To serve, place 2 cheese slice halves and one sausage link on the bottom half of each roll. Place on a broiler pan; broil 5 inches from heat until cheese is melted, 2 to 3 minutes. Spoon some roasted peppers onto sausages; add top halves of rolls. Serve with sauce from slow cooker in small bowls for dipping.

Serves 10

10 hot or sweet Italian pork sausage links
2 14-1/2 oz. cans fire-roasted diced tomatoes
28-oz. can crushed tomatoes
1 T. balsamic vinegar
6 cloves garlic, minced
2 t. dried basil
1 t. dried oregano
1/2 t. red pepper flakes
1/2 t. salt
1/2 t. pepper
10 slices provolone cheese, halved
10 French-style rolls or hoagie buns, split
Garnish: roasted red peppers

AUNTIE B'S BBQ ROAST SANDWICHES

BETHI HENDRICKSON
DANVILLE, PA

This recipe is a favorite for quick suppers or large groups. You can use a pork roast instead of beef in this recipe too...both are fantastic. Serve on hearty rolls and you have a winner!

3 to 4-lb. beef chuck
  roast
1 c. tomato juice
1/4 c. Worcestershire
  sauce
1 T. white vinegar
1 t. dry mustard
1 t. chili powder
1/4 t. garlic powder
hearty rolls, split

Spray a slow cooker with non-stick vegetable spray; add roast and set aside. In a small bowl, combine remaining ingredients except rolls. Stir until mixed well; pour mixture over roast. Cover and cook on low setting for 8 to 10 hours, or on high setting for 5 to 6 hours, until roast is very tender. Shred roast with 2 forks. Serve beef on rolls, drizzled with a little of the sauce from slow cooker.

Serves 10-12

MEATBALL HOAGIES

VIRGINIA WATSON
SCRANTON, PA

Hoagies, submarines, grinders, po' boys...whatever you call 'em, just call us for dinner!

In a large bowl, combine beef, bread crumbs, egg, onion, Parmesan cheese, salt and Worcestershire sauce. Using your hands, mix just until combined. Form into one-inch meatballs. Cook meatballs in a large skillet, turning occasionally, until browned on all sides. Remove meatballs to a slow cooker; top with pasta sauce. Cover and cook on low setting for about 2 hours, stirring after one hour. To serve, spoon several meatballs into each bun; top with a spoonful of sauce and a slice of cheese.

Serves 6 to 8

1 lb. lean ground beef
1/2 c. Italian-flavored dry bread crumbs
1 egg, beaten
2 T. onion, minced
1 T. grated Parmesan cheese
1 t. salt
1 t. Worcestershire sauce
32-oz. jar pasta sauce
hoagie rolls, split
Garnish: sliced mozzarella cheese

PROSCIUTTO, BRIE & APPLE PANINI

KATIE MAJESKE
DENVER, PA

This is one of our favorite sandwiches. It's great in the fall or winter with a cup of creamy tomato soup.

1/4 c. butter, softened

1 green onion, finely chopped

1/2 t. lemon juice

1/4 t. Dijon mustard

4 slices sourdough bread

3/4 lb. prosciutto or deli ham, thinly sliced

1/2 lb. brie cheese, cut into 4 pieces and rind removed

1 Granny Smith apple, peeled, cored and thinly sliced

In a bowl, beat butter until creamy. Stir in onion, lemon juice and mustard until smooth. Spread half the butter mixture on one side of 2 bread slices; place butter-side down on a heated panini maker or griddle. Top with prosciutto or ham, cheese and apple slices. Top with another slice of bread, spreading remaining butter on the outside. Cook until toasted and cheese is melted.

Serves 2

PEPPERONI PIZZA BURGERS

JANICE WOODS
NORTHERN CAMBRIA, PA

My family just loves pizza and burgers, so this makes for a great change at mealtime.

In a large bowl, combine beef, sausage and seasoning. Mix well; form into 6 patties. Heat a large skillet over medium-high heat. Add patties and cook to desired doneness, about 4 minutes per side. Reduce heat to low. When patties are nearly done, top each patty with 2 slices cheese and 5 to 6 slices pepperoni. Cover skillet; continue cooking until done, cheese is melted and pepperoni is warmed through. Spread cut sides of rolls with softened butter. In a separate skillet over medium heat, toast rolls until crisp and golden. Spread cut sides of rolls with sauce; sprinkle with Parmesan cheese. Place patties on bun bottoms; add tops. Serve immediately.

Serves 6

- 1-1/2 lbs. lean ground beef
- 1/2 lb. Italian ground pork sausage
- 1/2 t. Italian seasoning
- 12 slices mozzarella and/or provolone cheese
- 3-oz. pkg. sliced pepperoni
- 6 kaiser rolls, split
- softened butter to taste
- 3/4 c. marinara or pizza sauce, warmed
- grated Parmesan cheese to taste

HUNGARIAN BARBECUED WIENERS

MARCIA SHAFFER
CONNEAUT LAKE, PA

This recipe was handed down to me by my 82-year-old neighbor who is Hungarian. Every time I serve these wieners, I celebrate our friendship of over 40 years. They're a favorite on the 4th of July... so easy for kids to serve themselves when they come back from swimming in the lake. Happy eating!

2 T. butter

1 lb. hot dogs

1/3 c. green pepper, finely chopped

1/3 c. onion, finely chopped

10-3/4 oz. can tomato soup

2 T. brown sugar, packed

1 T. Worcestershire sauce

1 T. vinegar

1 T. mustard

8 hot dog buns, split

Melt butter in a skillet over medium heat. Add hot dogs, green pepper and onion; cook until hot dogs are browned. Stir in remaining ingredients. Cover; simmer for 30 minutes, stirring occasionally. Serve hot dogs on buns, topped with some of the sauce from skillet.

Serves 8

DEBBIE'S SAVORY ROAST SANDWICHES

DEBBIE FULS
FURNACE, PA

This recipe is one I make for out-of-town guests.

Place roast in a slow cooker; set aside. Mix together remaining ingredients except rolls; pour over roast. Cover and cook on low setting for 5 to 6 hours. Remove roast from slow cooker; shred with 2 forks. Return shredded meat to slow cooker; heat through and serve on rolls.

Serves 10 to 12

3 to 4-lb. beef or pork roast
14-oz. bottle catsup
1/2 c. taco sauce
1 onion, chopped
2 cloves garlic, pressed
2 T. brown sugar, packed
2 T. Worcestershire sauce
1 T. vinegar
1/8 t. dried oregano
1/8 t. dry mustard
1/8 t. pepper
10 to 12 hard rolls, split

DINNERTIME CONVERSATION

Pennsylvania is one of the few U.S. states that is a commonwealth, which has no legal meaning but emphasizes the role of the people in the state's government. (The others are Kentucky, Virginia and Massachusets.)

TAILGATE SANDWICH RING

CRYSTAL VOGEL
SPRINGDALE, PA

I make this for all my tailgating parties...my husband and friends request it all the time.

2 11-oz. tubes refrigerated French bread dough

1/2 lb. bacon, crisply cooked and crumbled

3/4 c. mayonnaise

1 T. green onion, chopped

1/2 lb. deli sliced turkey

1/2 lb. deli sliced ham

1/2 lb. sliced provolone cheese

2 tomatoes, sliced

2 c. lettuce, chopped

Spray a Bundt® pan with non-stick vegetable spray. Place both tubes of dough into pan, seam-side up, joining ends together to form one large ring. Pinch edges to seal tightly. Lightly spray top of dough with non-stick vegetable spray. Bake at 350 degrees for 40 to 45 minutes, until golden. Carefully turn out; cool completely. Combine bacon, mayonnaise and onion; mix well. Slice bread horizontally. Spread half the bacon mixture over bottom half of bread. Top with turkey, ham and provolone. Place on an ungreased baking sheet. Bake at 350 degrees until cheese melts. Top with tomatoes and lettuce. Spread remaining bacon mixture on top half; place over lettuce. Slice into wedges.

Serves 8

ROAST BEEF & HERBED CHEESE SANDWICHES

JUDI TOWNER
CLARKS SUMMIT, PA

These easy, delicious sandwiches are guaranteed to please any crowd! I've served them on various types of bread for ladies' bridal and baby shower luncheons...also served them on hard rolls at Super Bowl parties, and men love them too! I made them for my young grandsons, and they ate them up and asked for more. The cheese spread even makes a great dip for crackers and veggies.

In a bowl, combine all ingredients except beef and bread. Blend well with an electric mixer on low speed until smooth. Cover and chill in refrigerator if not using immediately. To serve, spread generously on bread or rolls; top with slices of roast beef.

Serves 4

8-oz. pkg. cream cheese, softened
1 T. lemon juice
1/2 t. garlic powder
1/2 t. dried basil
1/2 t. dill weed
1/2 t. dried parsley
1/2 t. celery salt
1/4 t. pepper
1 lb. thinly sliced deli roast beef
sliced rye bread or hard rolls

BRILLIANT BRICK SANDWICHES

LINDA KILGORE
KITTANNING, PA

This is my husband's recipe. One day he told the kids and me that he was making "brick sandwiches" for supper. The three of us just thought, OK, this better be good! Well...I believe it was the best sandwich I ever ate. The brick flattens the sandwich and cooks all the ingredients together. Absolutely delicious!

12 thick slices Italian bread
1 lb. deli baked ham, thinly sliced
1 lb. Swiss cheese, thinly sliced
1 onion, thinly sliced
1 tomato, thinly sliced
1/2 to 1 c. shredded lettuce
2 to 3 T. mayonnaise
1 T. olive oil

Wrap a clean new brick in aluminum foil. Place brick on an electric griddle; preheat over medium-high heat. Layer 6 bread slices with remaining ingredients except mayonnaise and oil. Spread one side of remaining bread slices with mayonnaise; close sandwiches. Brush outsides of sandwiches with oil. Place one sandwich on hot griddle; set the brick on top of the sandwich. Cook until sandwich is golden on both sides. Repeat with remaining sandwiches.

Serves 6

MOM'S HOT TURKEY SANDWICHES

KATIE MAJESKE
DENVER, PA

These sandwiches are so good...the recipe has been in our family for a long time! They're always a hit, and they're easy to make. Often I'll buy a turkey breast and roast it so I can prepare this the following day.

Combine all ingredients except buns in a large slow cooker. Cover and cook on low setting for 3 to 4 hours, until bubbly and cheese is melted. Stir; spoon onto buns.

Serves 12 to 16

8 c. cooked turkey, cubed

1 to 1-1/2 c. pasteurized process cheese spread, cubed

1 c. turkey or chicken broth

10-3/4 oz. can cream of mushroom or chicken soup

12 to 16 sandwich buns, split

TERIYAKI STEAK SUBS

VIRGINIA WATSON
SCRANTON, PA

We really enjoy these sandwiches at all our winter tailgating parties. They're great for an easy dinner too.

1/2 c. onion, chopped
1/2 c. soy sauce
1/4 c. red wine or beef broth
1 T. fresh ginger, peeled and grated
2 t. garlic, minced
1 T. sugar
3 lbs. beef round steak, cut crosswise into thirds
8 to 10 sub buns, split
Garnish: thinly sliced onion

In a bowl, combine all ingredients except beef, buns and garnish. Layer beef pieces in a slow cooker, spooning some of the onion mixture over each piece. Cover and cook on low setting for 6 to 7 hours, until beef is tender. Remove beef to a platter, reserving cooking liquid in slow cooker. Let beef stand several minutes before thinly slicing. To serve, place sliced beef on buns; top with sliced onion and some of the reserved cooking liquid.

Serves 8 to 10

CHILI DOG WRAPS

JEN STOUT
BLANDON, PA

These are great for the kids!

Warm tortillas as directed on package. Place one hot dog and 3 tablespoons chili on each tortilla. Roll up tortillas; place seam-side down in a greased 13"x9" baking pan. Spoon salsa over tortillas. Cover and bake at 350 degrees for 20 minutes. Sprinkle with cheese and bake, uncovered, about 5 minutes longer, or until cheese has melted.

Serves 10

10 6 or 8-inch flour or corn tortillas
10 hot dogs
16-oz. can chili
16-oz. jar salsa
1 c. shredded Cheddar or Monterey Jack cheese

TANGY TERIYAKI SANDWICHES

KELLY ALDERSON
ERIE, PA

What a combination of flavors...what a winner!

1-1/2 lbs. skinless turkey thighs
1/2 c. teriyaki baste and glaze sauce
3 T. orange marmalade
1/4 t. pepper
4 hoagie buns, split

Combine all ingredients except buns in a slow cooker; cover and cook on low setting for 9 to 10 hours. Remove turkey and shred meat, discarding bones; return to slow cooker. Cover and cook on high setting for 10 to 15 minutes, until sauce is thickened. Serve on hoagie buns.

Serves 4

DINNERTIME CONVERSATION

Bob Hoffman of York is hailed the world round as the Father of Weightlifting. Hoffman started York Barbell Corp. in 1932 and preached the gospel of physical fitness throughout his life as an U.S. Olympic coach, businessman and philanthropist.

CHICKEN-APPLE SLIDERS

KATIE MAJESKE
DENVER, PA

I love slider sandwiches! They are just the right size, especially when paired with salads and sides. This is one of our favorites.

In a large bowl, combine apple, celery and seasonings; toss to mix. Add honey, chicken and half of bacon. Stir until combined; do not overmix. Form into 8 small patties. Grill or pan-fry patties about 4 minutes on each side, until chicken is no longer pink. If desired, top with a piece of cheese during the last few minutes of cooking. Place patties on rolls; top with remaining bacon and other toppings, as desired.

Serves 8

1 Granny Smith apple, cored and shredded

1/4 c. celery, finely chopped

1/2 t. poultry seasoning

1/4 t. pepper

1/4 t. salt

2 T. honey

1 lb. ground chicken

8 slices bacon, crisply cooked, crumbled and divided

Optional: 2 slices favorite cheese, quartered

8 mini rolls, toasted and split

Garnish: mayonnaise, shredded lettuce, sliced tomato and onion

BETH'S STUFFED BURGERS

HEATHER STRAUSS
WAYNESBORO, PA

My sister Beth developed this recipe one day on a whim...it's been a family favorite ever since!

2 lbs. lean ground beef
2 eggs, beaten
1/2 c. dry bread crumbs
1/2 c. onion, finely chopped
1/2 c. finely shredded Cheddar cheese
1/4 to 1/2 c. barbecue sauce
8 hamburger buns, split and toasted
Garnish: favorite toppings

In a large bowl, mix all ingredients except rolls and garnish. Do not overmix. Form into 8 flattened patties. Coat a skillet with non-stick vegetable spray; heat over medium heat. If grilling, place aluminum foil on a rack and coat well with non-stick spray. Add patties and cook for about 5 to 6 minutes on each side, until juices run clear; don't move or press down on patties. Serve patties on toasted buns with desired toppings.

Serves 8

BARBECUED BEEF

MISSY ABBOTT
HICKORY, PA

I was at a Christmas party where the hostess served barbecued beef but preferred not to share her secrets. So I came up with my own recipe, which my husband likes even better! Now everyone asks for my recipe which I gladly share. I have found a pork roast can be used with equally delicious results. It pairs nicely with scalloped potatoes or mac & cheese.

Place roast in a 6-quart slow cooker; add water. Cover and cook on high setting for about 6 hours. Meanwhile, combine remaining ingredients except buns in a bowl; cover and refrigerate. Once roast has cooked, remove to a platter; shred roast with a fork. Drain liquid from slow cooker; add shredded beef. Pour sauce over top; stir. Cover and continue cooking on high setting for 1-1/2 to 2 hours longer. Serve shredded beef on buns.

Serves 12 to 15

5-lb. beef rump roast, fat trimmed
2 c. water
10-3/4 oz. can tomato soup
1 c. brown sugar, packed
1/4 c. catsup
1/4 c. butter, melted
2 T. spicy brown mustard
2 T. smoke-flavored cooking sauce
2 T. lemon juice
1 T. Worcestershire sauce
1-1/4 t. granulated garlic
sandwich buns, split

MY BEST BEAN & BACON SOUP

CAROL DELOZIER
EAST FREEDOM, PA

I've always loved the flavor of navy beans with ham or bacon. The Pennsylvania Dutch-style rivels are fun and easy to make. Enjoy!

1 lb. bacon, cut into 1-inch pieces
2 15-1/2 oz. cans Great Northern beans
4 c. water
salt to taste
3 eggs, beaten
3/4 to 1 c. all-purpose flour

In a skillet over medium heat, cook bacon to desired crispness; drain and set aside. Pour undrained beans into a large saucepan; stir in water, bacon and salt to taste. Simmer over medium heat for 30 minutes, stirring often. To make rivels, mix eggs with enough flour to make a slightly thickened batter. Drop batter by spoonfuls into boiling broth. Cover and cook about 15 to 20 minutes longer.

Serves 6

ITALIAN HAMBURGERS

GLADYS BREHM
QUAKERTOWN, PA

This is a great quick & easy recipe for entertaining family & friends at cookouts. I have had several friends request it once they tasted my burgers. It's such a good feeling to be able to share your recipes with folks who enjoy your cooking!

In a large bowl, combine all ingredients except buns. Mix well and form into 12 to 14 patties. Grill to preferred doneness. Serve on buns.

Serves 12 to 14

2 to 3 slices bacon, crisply cooked and crumbled

3 lbs. ground beef

7-oz. pkg. Italian salad dressing mix

2 eggs, beaten

1 c. Italian-flavored dry bread crumbs

1 c. shredded mozzarella cheese

12 to 14 hamburger buns, split

EVERYONE'S FAVORITE VEGETABLE SOUP

MARCEL BEERS
EASTON, PA

Like a vegetable garden in a soup bowl...even my one-year-old likes it!

1 lb. stew beef cubes
1 T. oil
4 potatoes, peeled and diced
16-oz. pkg. frozen peas
16-oz. pkg. frozen corn
16-oz. pkg. baby carrots
2 12-oz. jars beef gravy
2 15-oz. cans tomato sauce
salt and pepper to taste

In a skillet over medium heat, brown beef in oil; drain. Add potatoes to skillet; cook until softened. Combine beef mixture and remaining ingredients in a slow cooker. Cover and cook on low setting for 8 hours, or until tender, stirring occasionally.

Serves 8

PRESENTATION

Add the words "Today's Menu" across the top of a small blackboard with acrylic paint. Hang it in the kitchen and update it daily with chalk... everyone is sure to hurry to the dinner table when they know what's for dinner!

SCOTT'S HAM & PEAR SANDWICHES

KATHY MAJESKE
DENVER, PA

My brother, who is an amazing cook, gave me this recipe. The spiced butter makes it especially crispy and good!

Spread each bread slice with a thin layer of Spiced Butter. On each of 4 slices, place one slice of cheese; layer evenly with ham and pears. Top with remaining bread slices and press together gently. Spread the outside of the sandwiches with Spiced Butter. Heat a large skillet over medium-high heat and cook until crisp and golden, about 5 minutes on each side.

Spiced Butter: Combine all ingredients until smooth and evenly mixed.

Serves 4

8 slices sourdough bread

4 slices Swiss cheese

1-1/4 lbs. sliced deli ham

15-oz. can pear halves, drained and thinly sliced

SPICED BUTTER

1 c. butter, softened

2 t. pumpkin pie spice

1 t. ground coriander

1 t. ground ginger

1 t. salt

BACKYARD BIG SOUTH-OF-THE-BORDER BURGERS

PAULA MARCHESI
AUBURN, PA

Every time I bite into a scrumptious, juicy burger cooked on an outside grill, I'm a kid again, at our picnic table with family & friends.

4-oz. can chopped green chiles, drained

1/4 c. picante sauce

12 round buttery crackers, crushed

4-1/2 t. chili powder

1 T. ground cumin

1/2 t. smoke-flavored cooking sauce

1/2 t. salt

1/2 t. pepper

2 lbs. lean ground beef

1/2 lb. ground pork sausage

6 slices Pepper Jack cheese

6 sesame seed hamburger buns, split

Garnish: lettuce leaves, sliced tomato

In a large bowl, combine first 8 ingredients. Crumble beef and sausage over mixture and mix well. Form into 6 patties. Grill, covered, over medium heat for 5 to 7 minutes on each side, or until no longer pink. Top with cheese. Grill until cheese is melted. Grill buns, cut-side down, for one to 2 minutes, or until toasted. Serve burgers on buns, garnished as desired.

Serves 6

HONEY-BARBECUED PORK

CAROL SMITH
WEST LAWN, PA

This slow-cooker recipe is my mom's. Try it on mini buns for sliders!

Place pork in a slow cooker. Add onions, barbecue sauce and honey. Cover and cook on low setting for 6 to 8 hours. Use 2 forks to shred roast; mix well. Serve on rolls.

Serves 6 to 8

2 to 3-lb. pork roast
2 onions, chopped
12-oz. bottle barbecue sauce
1/4 c. honey
6 to 8 sandwich rolls, split

BEEF STEW & BISCUITS

JOCELYN MEDINA
PHOENIXVILLE, PA

This tried & true one-pot meal is perfect for Sunday dinner.

In a skillet, brown beef and onion; drain. Add seasonings, mixed vegetables and tomato sauce; mix well. Cover and simmer for 5 minutes. Fold in cheese cubes; pour into an ungreased 2-quart casserole dish. Arrange biscuits on top. Bake, uncovered, at 375 degrees for 25 minutes, or until biscuits are golden.

Serves 4 to 6

1 lb. ground beef
1/4 c. onion, chopped
1/4 t. dried basil
1/8 t. pepper
3-1/2 c. frozen or canned mixed vegetables
2 8-oz. cans tomato sauce
1 c. sharp Cheddar cheese, cubed
12-oz. tube refrigerated biscuits

SLOPPY COWBOYS

RACHEL KOWASIC
CONNELLSVILLE, PA

I found a recipe for Sloppy Joes, but they weren't quite what I wanted, so I turned them into my own special type of Sloppy Joe.

2 lbs. lean ground beef
1/2 t. dried oregano
1/2 t. dried basil
1/2 t. onion powder
1/3 t. garlic powder
0.7-oz. pkg. Italian salad dressing mix
1 T. red wine vinegar
1 t. Worcestershire sauce
1/3 c. catsup
sandwich buns
1/2 lb. provolone cheese, sliced

Brown beef in a large skillet over medium heat; drain. Add remaining ingredients except buns and cheese and mix well. Reduce heat to low; simmer until heated through and slightly thickened. Serve on buns, topped with a slice of provolone cheese.

Serves 6 to 8

SUPER-EASY SAUSAGE SANDWICHES

BETH HARMAN
HEGINS, PA

Most of my family are hunters, so I always use homemade venison sausage, but any sausage will do. These sausages taste great on a hearty sandwich roll.

Place sausage links in a slow cooker. Layer peppers and onion over links; spoon sauce over all. Season with pepper. Cover and cook on low setting for 6 hours. Place sausages in rolls and top with peppers, onions and sauce from slow cooker.

Serves 6 to 8

1-1/2 lbs. Italian pork sausage links
2 green peppers, sliced
1 onion, sliced
24-oz. can spaghetti sauce
pepper to taste
6 to 8 sandwich rolls, split

SWEET & SAVORY BEEF SANDWICHES

LISA SCHNECK
LEHIGHTON, PA

I love the simplicity of my slow cooker...just add ingredients, turn it on, and a few hours later this delicious, no-fuss meal awaits my hungry family.

Stir together beer, sugar and catsup in a slow cooker. Add roast and spoon mixture over top. Cover and cook on low setting for 7 to 8 hours. Remove roast and shred; return to juices in slow cooker. Serve shredded beef on rolls for sandwiches, topped with pepper slices if desired.

Serves 6 to 8

12-oz. can beer or non-alcoholic beer
1 c. brown sugar, packed
24-oz. bottle catsup
3 to 4-lb. boneless beef roast
6 to 8 split Kaiser rolls
Optional: banana pepper slices

PHILLY CHEESESTEAK

KELLEY NICHOLSON
PITTSBURGH, PA

This is one of my husband's favorite sandwiches. Every time I make it, he says it takes him down memory lane to his college days in PA.

4 Hoagie Rolls 2 T butter, softened

1 garlic clove, minced

2 T Olive oil, divided

1 large sweet onion, sliced

1 green pepper, sliced

1 lb Ribeye steak trimmed and very thinly sliced

1/2 tsp salt to taste

1/2 tsp pepper to taste

8 slices mild provolone cheese

Slice hoagie rolls 3/4 of the way through with a serrated knife. In a small bowl, stir together softened butter and garlic; spread onto cut sides of rolls. Toast buttered side of rolls on a large skillet or griddle over medium heat until golden; set aside. Add one tablespoon oil to pan and sauté pepper until tender. Add onion; cook for about __ minutes, until caramelized. Transfer onion mixture to a bowl. Increase to high heat and add remaining oil. Spread sliced steak in an even layer. Let brown for a couple of minutes; flip steak and and season with salt and pepper. Sauté until steak is fully cooked; stir in caramelized onion mixture. Divide evenly into 4 portions. Layer 2 slices of cheese in each bun; top with steak mixture. Serve warm

Serves 4

BUFFALO CHICKEN SOUP

KRISTI BESTWICK
BUTLER, PA

This slow-cooker recipe is perfect for those cold days when you just can't get warm. This soup is guaranteed to warm you up from the inside out! I use a rotisserie chicken to speed up the process.

Combine all ingredients in a 5-quart slow cooker; stir well. Cover and cook on low setting for 4 to 5 hours. If desired, garnish individual servings with cheese.

Serves 12 to 15

6 c. milk

3 10-3/4 oz. cans cream of chicken soup

3 c. cooked chicken, shredded

1 c. sour cream

1/4 to 3/4 c. hot pepper sauce, to taste

2 T. ranch salad dressing mix

Optional: shredded Cheddar cheese

BUMSTEADS

CAROL MACKLEY
MANHEIM, PA

This is one of the Depression-era recipes my mother used to make. They were simple and inexpensive, but we thought they were really delicious...I bet you will too!

Combine all ingredients except buns; spoon into buns. Arrange on an aluminum foil-lined baking sheet. Bake at 350 degrees for 15 to 20 minutes, or until heated through and cheese is melted.

Serves 8

3 eggs, hard-boiled, peeled and chopped

1/4 lb. white American cheese, diced

6-oz. can tuna, drained

2 T. green pepper, chopped

2 T. green olives with pimentos, chopped

2 T. sweet pickle relish

1/2 c. mayonnaise

8 hot dog buns, split

THE ULTIMATE SLOW-COOKER KIELBASA SOUP

JUDY LANGE
IMPERIAL, PA

This is a terrific cold-weather soup...warms you right up after a hockey game!

16-oz. pkg. frozen mixed vegetables

6-oz. can tomato paste

1 onion, chopped

3 potatoes, diced

1-1/2 to 2 lbs. Kielbasa sausage, thinly sliced

4 qts. water

Optional: chopped fresh parsley

Combine all ingredients except parsley in a slow cooker. Cover and cook on low setting 10 to 12 hours. Garnish individual servings with parsley, if desired.

Serves 8

HALFTIME PORK SANDWICHES

JOANNA NICOLINE-HAUGHEY
BERWYN, PA

Come and get it...the sandwiches are always ready to go at halftime!

3 to 4-lb. boneless center-cut pork loin

4 to 5 cloves garlic

2 to 3 T. olive oil

salt and pepper to taste

6 to 8 kaiser rolls, split

7-oz. jar roasted red peppers, drained

1/2 lb. sliced provolone cheese

Make 4 to 5 tiny slits in pork loin with a knife tip; insert garlic cloves. Place pork loin in a slow cooker. Drizzle with olive oil; sprinkle with salt and pepper. Cover and cook on low setting for 8 to 9 hours. Shred pork with 2 forks. Serve on kaiser rolls, topped with red peppers and cheese.

Serves 6 to 8

TOMATO-TORTELLINI SOUP

DIANE BAILEY
RED LION, PA

Mamma mia! This is oh-so satisfying and really easy to put together... ready in about 20 minutes.

Melt margarine in a saucepan over medium heat; add garlic. Sauté for 2 minutes; stir in broth and tortellini. Bring to a boil; reduce heat. Mix in Parmesan cheese, salt and pepper; simmer until tortellini is tender. Stir in spinach, tomatoes and tomato sauce; simmer for 5 minutes, until heated through.

Serves 8 to 10

1 T. margarine

3 cloves garlic, minced

3 10-1/2 oz. cans chicken broth

8-oz. pkg. cheese-filled tortellini, uncooked

1/4 c. grated Parmesan cheese salt and pepper to taste

2/3 c. frozen chopped spinach, thawed and drained

14-1/2 oz. can Italian stewed tomatoes

1/2 c. tomato sauce

NOT YOUR MOTHER'S TUNA SALAD

MEL CHENCHARICK
JULIAN, PA

This delicious tuna salad can be served on sliced bread, in pita pockets or spooned into sliced tomatoes. It can even be used to fill deviled eggs...stir in the chopped yolks along with the tuna. Use low-fat mayonnaise and fat-free cheese, if you like. A great, versatile recipe for a ladies' luncheon!

7-oz. can white tuna in water, drained and flaked

6 to 8 T. mayonnaise or mayonnaise-style salad dressing

1 T. shredded Parmesan cheese

3 T. sweet pickle relish

1/8 t. dried minced onion

1 t. dried parsley

1 t. dill weed

1/8 t. garlic powder

In a bowl, stir together tuna and mayonnaise or salad dressing. Add Parmesan cheese, pickle relish and onion; mix well. Season with parsley, dill and garlic powder. Cover and chill for at least one hour before serving.

Serves 4